Your Brain

Ted Martell

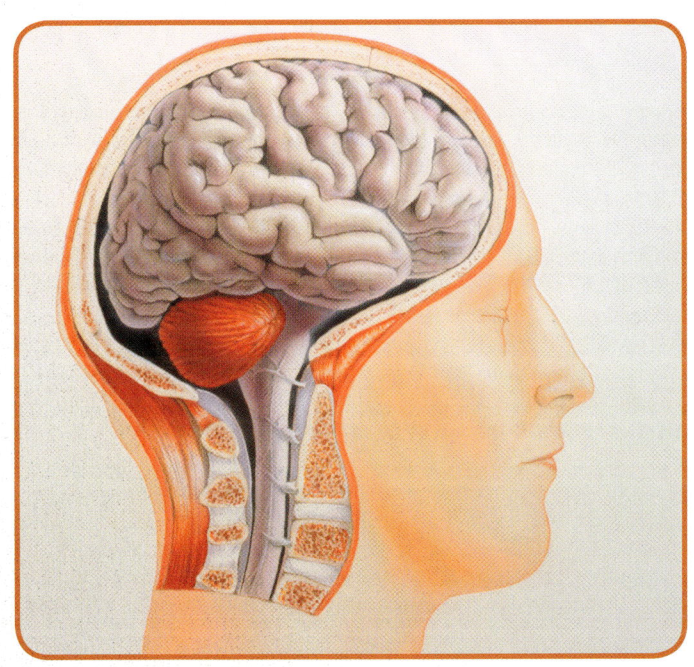

SCHOLASTIC INC.

NEW YORK • TORONTO • LONDON • AUCKLAND • SYDNEY
MEXICO CITY • NEW DELHI • HONG KONG • BUENOS AIRES

ISBN-13: 978-0-545-06095-0/ ISBN-10: 0-545-06095-8

Photos Credits:
Cover: © Stockbyte/Getty Images; title page: © David Gifford/Photo Researchers, Inc.; contents page, from top: © Brand New Images/Getty Images, © Bruce Laurance/Getty Images, © Guy Ryecart/Dorling Kindersley/Getty Images; page 4, left: © Brand New Images/Getty Images; page 4, right: © Jose Luis Pelaez Inc. (RF)/Blend Images/Corbis; page 5, top left: © Carl Schneider/Getty Images; page 5, top right: © Stockbyte (RF)/Getty Images; page 5, bottom left: © David Buffington (RF)/Getty Images; page 5, bottom right: © Jack Hollingsworth/Getty Images; page 6: © John M. Daugherty/Photo Researchers, Inc.; page 7: © Dorling Kindersley (RF)/Getty Images; page 8: © Bruce Laurance/Getty Images; page 9: © moodboard/Corbis; page 10: © 3D4Medical.com/Getty Images; page 11: © Dorling Kindersley/Getty Images; page 12: © Guy Ryecart/Dorling Kindersley/Getty Images; page 13: © Tom & Dee Ann McCarthy/Corbis; page 14: © Alistair Berg/Getty Images; page 15: © Dan Dalton (RF)/Digital Vision/Getty Images; back cover: © Tom & Dee Ann McCarthy/Corbis.

Photo research by Dwayne Howard
Design by Holly Grundon

12 11 10 9 8 7 6 5 4 3 2 1 8 9 10 11 12 13/0

Printed in the U.S.A.
First printing, September 2008

Contents

Chapter 1

What Is Your Brain?

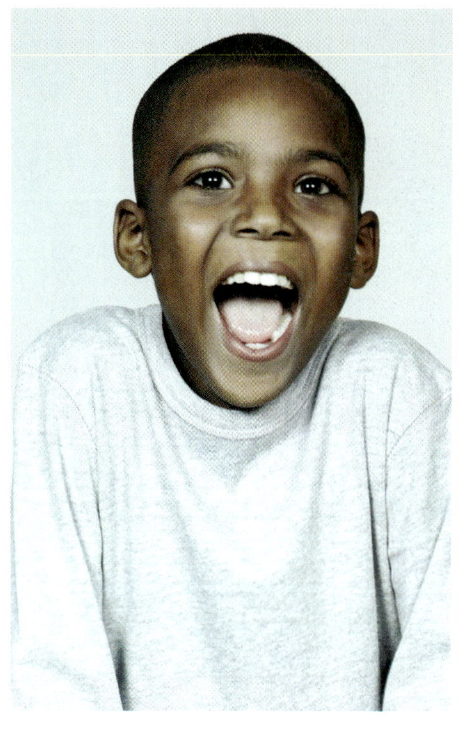

laugh

cry

You can do so many different things. You can laugh and cry.

run

jump

eat

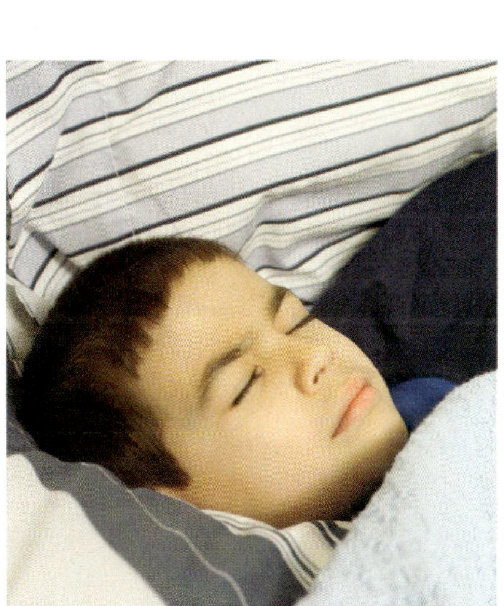

sleep

You can run and jump and eat and sleep.
How do you do all of these things?

The Human Brain

Fast Fact

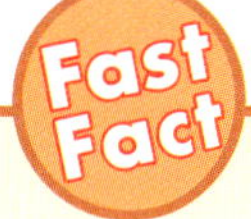

An adult's brain weighs about 3 pounds.

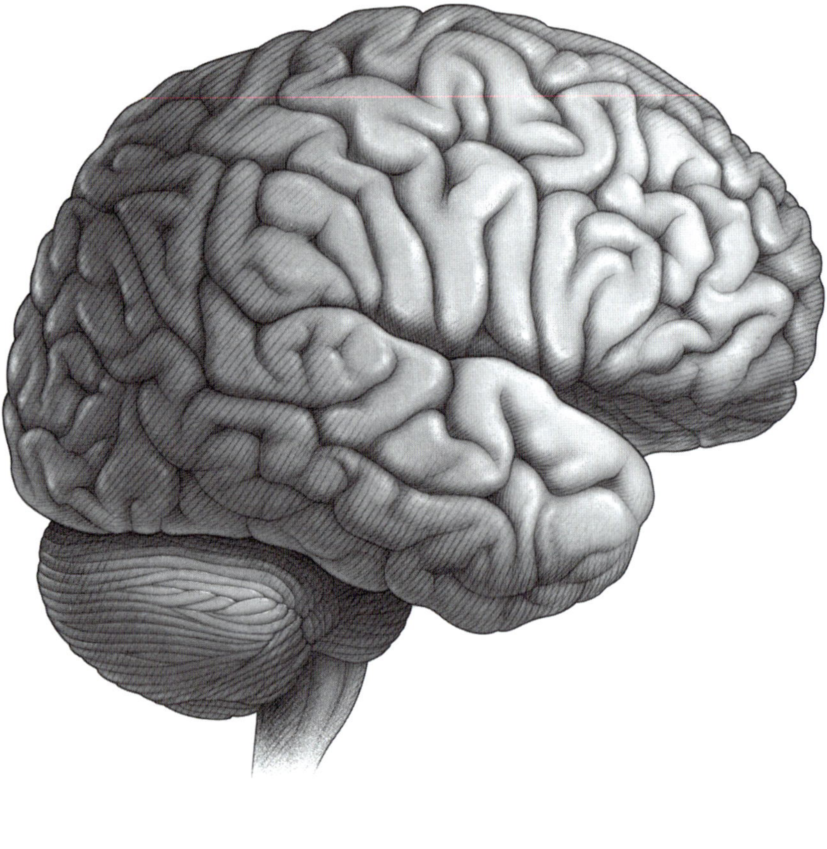

You do all of these things with your brain!
Your brain is soft and gray and wrinkly.
It looks like this.

Your Head

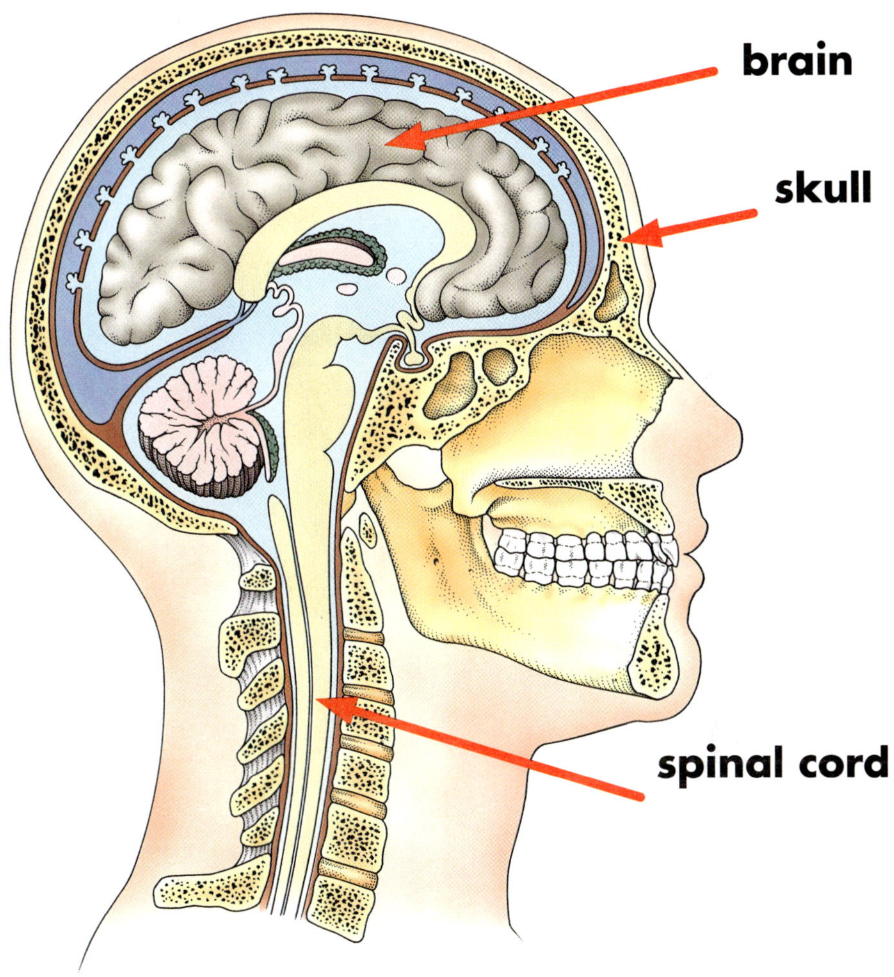

Your brain is inside your skull. Your skull **protects** it. Let's learn all about your brilliant brain!

Chapter 2

Your Body's Computer

Think of your brain as your body's computer. Your brain sends and receives **messages**. It tells your body what to do.

What happens when you see a delicious cupcake? Your eyes send a message to your brain. Then your brain tells your mouth to take a bite. Yum!

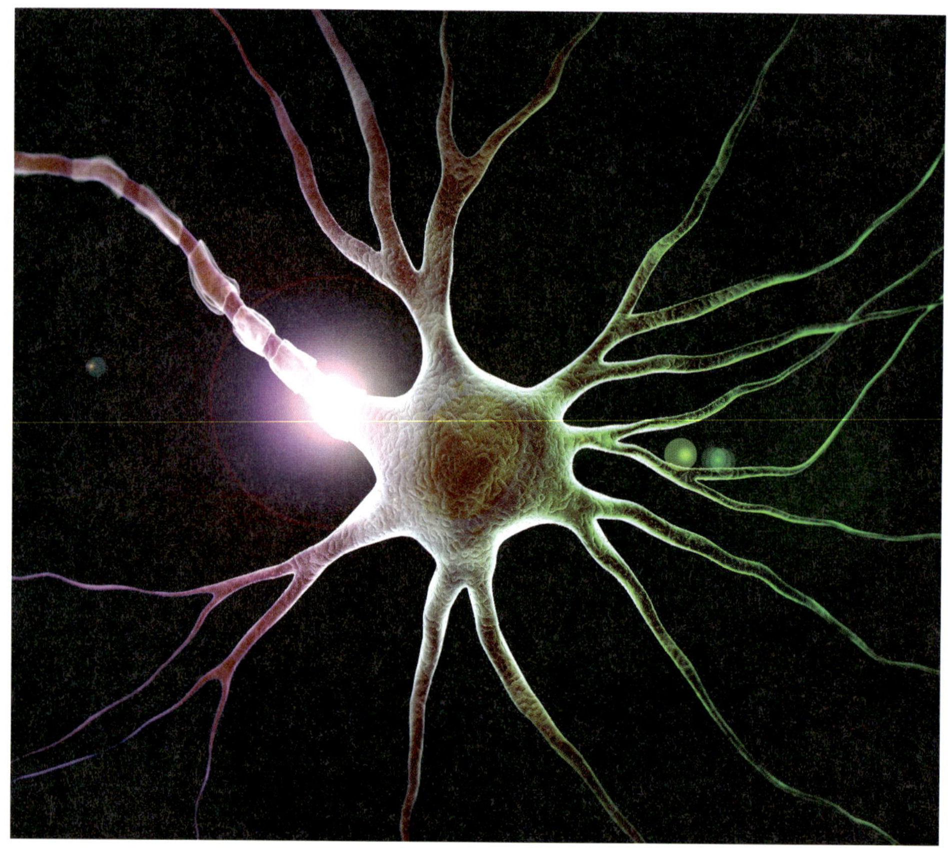

Under a microscope, a neuron looks like a star. You body has billions of them.

What happens when you stub your big toe? Tiny things called **neurons** send a message from your toe to your brain. Then your brain tells you that it hurts. Ouch!

Inside Your Body

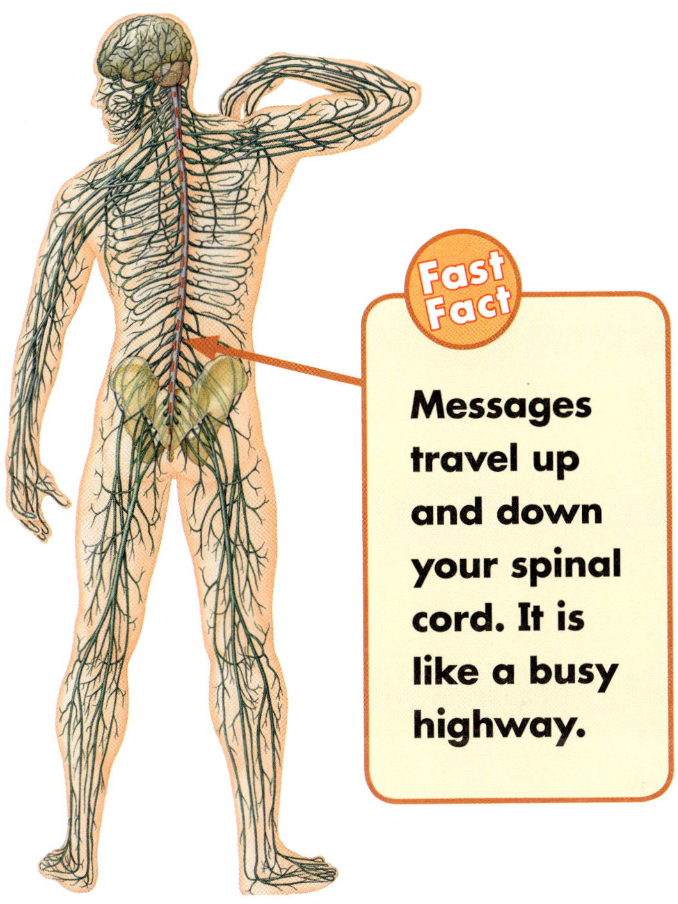

Fast Fact

Messages travel up and down your spinal cord. It is like a busy highway.

Neurons also tell your brain how things taste or feel. Zip! Zap! Messages are constantly traveling between your brain and body.

Chapter 3

Your Brain at Work

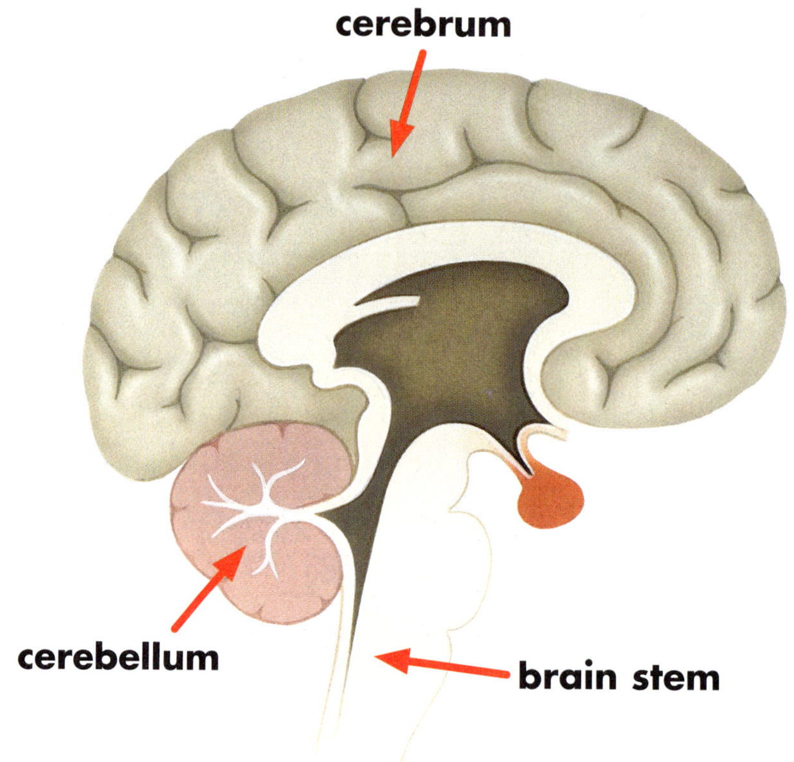

Your brain is divided into three main parts. Each of the parts has a different job to do.

Cerebrum Jobs

- reading
- writing
- talking
- drawing
- remembering
- paying attention

The **cerebrum** is the biggest part of your brain. It controls thinking. You use it to do math and remember the way home from school.

The **cerebellum** controls movement. You use it to jog and jump. You also use it to keep your balance when you walk on a log!

Brain Stem Jobs

- **breathing**
- **digesting food**
- **heartbeat**
- **blood flow**

The **brain stem** controls your breathing and heartbeat. These things happen **automatically** whether you are awake or asleep. Wow! Your brain sure is super!

Glossary

automatically (aw-tuh-**mat**-ik-lee): happens by itself without conscious thought

brain stem (**brayn** stem): part of the brain that controls involuntary functions

cerebellum (ser-uh-**bel**-uhm): part of the brain that controls coordination

cerebrum (suh-**ree**-bruhm): part of the brain that controls thinking and voluntary functions

message (**mess**-ij): information that is sent to someone or something

neurons (**nur**-ronz): nerve cells that send messages to and from the brain

protect (pruh-**tekt**): to keep safe from harm

Comprehension Questions

1. Can you name three things your brain helps you do?
2. Can you remember the three main parts of the brain?
3. Can you think of three great words to describe your brain?